Life on the Water

A COMMERCIAL FISHERMEN'S TALE ON LAKE SUPERIOR

JANET JOHNSON

Copyright © 2011 by Janet Johnson. 97066-JOHN
ISBN: Softcover   978-1-4653-3800-6

All rights reserved. No part of this book may be reproduced or transmitted in any form or by any means, electronic or mechanical, including photocopying, recording, or by any information storage and retrieval system, without permission in writing from the copyright owner.

To order additional copies of this book, contact:
Xlibris Corporation
1-888-795-4274
www.Xlibris.com
Orders@Xlibris.com

Introduction

This is the story of commercial fishing on Lake Superior. As with any occupation that relies on nature, it can be both destructive and rewarding. Commercial fishermen are a proud, hardworking, committed group of people. Their days are long. The work can be dangerous. But some say, that if you are born into a fishing family, it is in your blood. It is a part of you, of who you are. The lake becomes your master and you a slave to it.

It's mid-March, the ice is starting to break-up on the lake. Within a few weeks the two commercial fishing vessels should be able to start fishing. It all depends on the wind. The wind will move the ice back and forth, smashing and crashing it, until there is almost nothing left. A good nor-easter will create big waves that will pound on the remaining ice floes, breaking them into small enough pieces the sun can do the rest.

A good nor-easter is exactly what they need to break up the ice in the entry slip and harbor. If the ice can be broken up to the corner where the slip meets the harbor path, then it is the job of the fishing boat to break up the ice from their fishing dock to that corner.

This year the lake opened early, but the harbor ice was stubborn and not melting or moving. The fishermen were getting restless and decided to try to break out.

Just when the frozen winter bares down upon the north land for a long winter, they lay the boat up. They dock the fishing boats about ten feet from the dock and tie them off with big, three inch diameter ropes. The fishermen's first job in the spring was to get onto the boat, charge the battery, check and recheck the equipment, and move her next to, or as close to, the dock for fuel. The boat uses diesel fuel and wood for their potbelly stove.

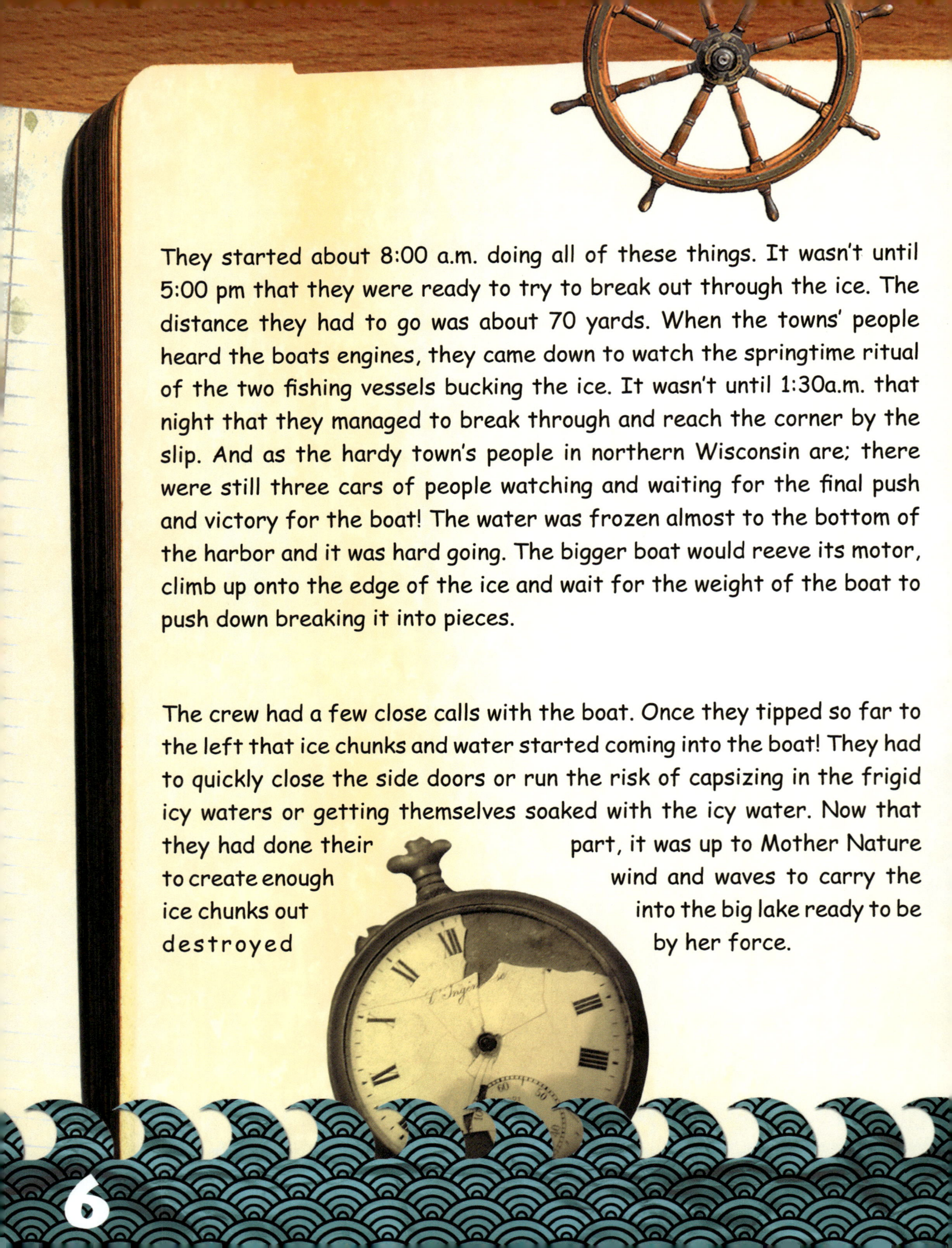

They started about 8:00 a.m. doing all of these things. It wasn't until 5:00 pm that they were ready to try to break out through the ice. The distance they had to go was about 70 yards. When the towns' people heard the boats engines, they came down to watch the springtime ritual of the two fishing vessels bucking the ice. It wasn't until 1:30a.m. that night that they managed to break through and reach the corner by the slip. And as the hardy town's people in northern Wisconsin are; there were still three cars of people watching and waiting for the final push and victory for the boat! The water was frozen almost to the bottom of the harbor and it was hard going. The bigger boat would reeve its motor, climb up onto the edge of the ice and wait for the weight of the boat to push down breaking it into pieces.

The crew had a few close calls with the boat. Once they tipped so far to the left that ice chunks and water started coming into the boat! They had to quickly close the side doors or run the risk of capsizing in the frigid icy waters or getting themselves soaked with the icy water. Now that they had done their part, it was up to Mother Nature to create enough wind and waves to carry the ice chunks out into the big lake ready to be destroyed by her force.

The fishing season on the South Shore of Lake Superior has started for another year.

The fishing boat, "Julie Ann", trying to break through the harbor ice by riding on top of the ice until it breaks from the weight.

Once free from the harbor ice, they can still get trapped in the ever moving lake ice that fills the bays. Open water is seen over the boat.

As the two fishing boats struggle to get free of the ice, a Laker sails by.

Two eagles are perched on the icy entrance to the harbor.

Beep! Beep! Beep! That's the sound of Jeff's alarm clock going off.. It is 3:30 in the morning. The stars are still shining and the crescent moon is lowering itself in the western sky. It is time for Jeff to get out of bed. Today, he is going to go fishing with his dad and brothers. This is not sport fishing, which you do just for fun and enjoyment, this is for work, a job, a demanding job. Jeff's dad is a commercial fisherman on Lake Superior.

Lake Superior is the farthest west of the five Great Lakes that make up part of the border between the United States and Canada. Jeff's family business in located on the south shore in the western part of Lake Superior.

The dark line by Duluth shows the south shore of Lake Superior.

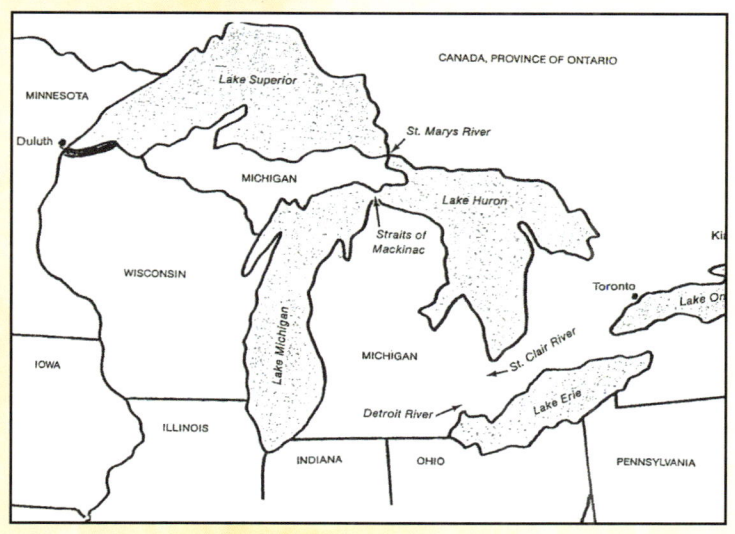

Jeff's great grandfather, Alick, came from Sweden to fish the Great Lakes. He first started fishing in Gills Rock, Wisconsin. When commercial fishing started to decline, Alick moved to the south shore of Lake Superior to fish with his three sons.

Jeff's grandfather, Everett, was one of these three sons. He fished with his father and uncle's for many years. In 1947, he branched out and extended his fishing business with the addition of smoke houses. He began smoking some of the fish, the smoked fish caught on and at one point, he had eight smoke houses by the harbor. Today, the one smoke house is located on the eastern side of the town and is larger and more modern than the original smoke houses.

Then Jeff's dad, Eric, started working for the fishing business. When he came back from college with three degrees; business, accounting, biology, he took over the family business. The name of Everett Fisheries was never changed and is still used today.

Jeff has four older brothers who have worked in the family business while they were growing up and in school. Now two of the brothers run most of the operation.

Jeff, who is eleven and in the fifth grade, is able to do more work. He started working when he was about eight years old. He did a lot of the time consuming work, the "grunt" work. He would stack wood and haul in wood for smoking, haul the garbage, clean the fish boxes, wash down the floors and any other jobs that the older boys did not want to do! Jeff likes working with his dad and brothers and it makes him feel good to be a helping part of the family business.

The boat they use for fishing is named the "Julie Ann" after Jeff's oldest sister. It is a 52 foot steel boat. There is a radar system on the boat to help them find their way in case of bad seas or fog. There is a fish finder on the boat too. This helps them find the biggest schools of fish and tells them how deep the fish are in the water. They need to know this so they know how deep to set their nets.

They have a small pot belly stove on the boat to keep them warm in the mornings when it is cold before the warmth of the sun can heat up the cold lake air.

In the bow, or front of the boat, they have a lifter. This is a hydraulic machine that helps them pull their nets full of fish in from the lake. When the nets are soggy and full of either fish or debris, they can get quite heavy. The lifter helps take off some of the weight by lifting the nets up into the side of the boat.

The fishing boat, JULIE ANN, returning to the harbor after a day on Lake Superior.

Today, Jeff gets to go on the lake for his first time. It is early April, the lake is calm and the forecast looks good for a safe day on the big lake. It is a good day for Jeff to try out his sealegs. Today, Jeff will help his dad lift chub nets. Chubs look like big minnows! The commercial fisherman on Lake Superior fish for many kinds of fish. They catch whitefish, trout, herring, chubs, and sometimes smelt.

The chubs, herring, and smelt are similar in shape and vary only in size. The trout can vary from lean trout which are good for eating to the fats which are a bigger, fatter fish and used mostly in smoking. The whitefish have a white meat and mild flavor.

Jeff's dad and other commercial fishermen on the big lakes fish with gill nets. A gill net looks like a volleyball or tennis net but much wider. It is made from many squares of nylon twine and sewn together. The size of the square depends on the size and type of fish they want to catch. The squares on a gill net that is used for chubs and herring is $2\frac{1}{2}$ to 3 inches on each side. The squares on a gill net that are used to catch large fish like trout, whitefish, and salmon are from 4 to 6 inches. They put these nets in boxes and then load the boxes onto the boat, but only the nets they need that day are loaded the rest are stored in a building called the "net shed."

The net shed is across the road from the fishing dock. This is the building where they store the unused nets and where they mend the nets in the winter.

A net box with a nylon net ready to be set in the lake.

Inside the net shed, a wood reel with a net in the process of getting mended.

Boxes of nets waiting to get mended.

In the winter, they spend many hours a day mending these nets that get torn from the waves, sticks and other materials in the lake. The big waves they get on Lake Superior can cause a lot of damage to their nets.

In the fall evenings, Jeff has to wind nylon thread around big plastic needles that they use to mend the torn nets. They do this by weaving the big needle wound with nylon thread back and forth and through the tears. They have to cut out the pieces in the net that are so torn they cannot save it.

It usually takes Jeff about one hour to put enough thread on one needle for it to be ready. He has to wind about 30 needles total.

A man using a needle to mend the net by sewing the nylon into the torn areas making more squares.

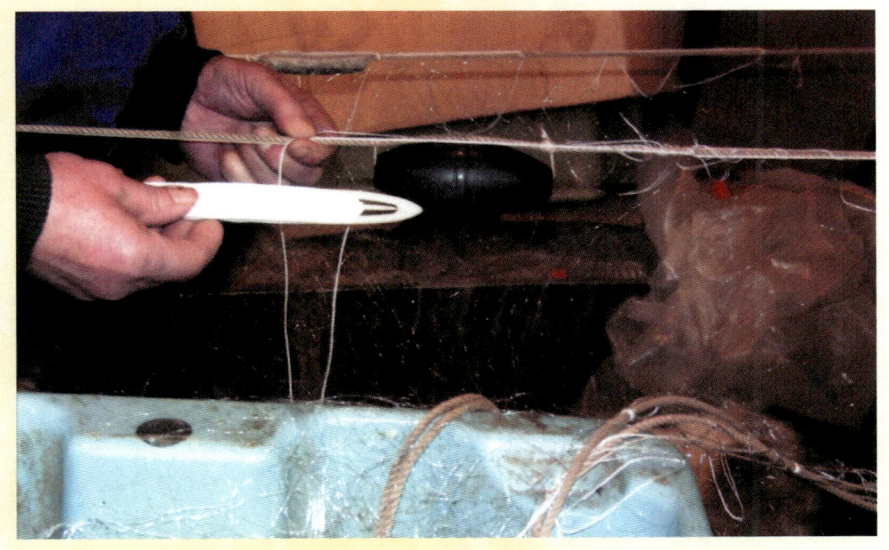

Jeff likes to help his dad as much as he can. He can work on week-ends in the Spring and Fall and he can work for awhile after school. He can work most days in the summer between swimming and baseball! They do not fish in the winter because it gets too cold and Lake Superior produces a lot of ice.

The lake does not usually freeze over because it is so big and deep the water stays warmer for a longer period of time. Lake Superior is the largest and deepest of the five Great Lakes.

Lake Superior gets very windy, wild and rough in the Fall. The "Gales of November" are what they call this time of year. It is a time when the wind blows extremely hard from the northeast. They call these winds "nor-easters". The winds can create waves up to 20 feet high. They look like waves one would see on an ocean! These waves have taken the lives of many good men and caused many big ore boats to capsize and sink.

Waves off the shore near Port Wing in early Fall shows the force of a nor-easter.

A fishing boat going out on the lake with sea gulls surrounding it.

Even on a semi-rough days, the boats have to go out.

Jeff and the crew are going out about six miles this morning. The ride on the Julie Ann will take them about 45 minutes. Now is a good time for Jeff to curl up in an empty fish box and take a nap! Jeff's dad will monitor the radar that is on the boat to help them find their nets.

Once they get close, they can spot them by the big buoys floating in the water. There is a buoy tied on each end of their net. They use a small chain to connect the buoys to the net. The buoys are used for a couple of reasons: it helps them find their nets, it tells other fishermen whose nets they are, and it warns boaters that there are nets in the water in this area.

When the crew is ready to lift the nets, they usually start from the inside, which is the buoy closest to shore, and lift or pull the nets into the boat working their way away from the shore. They lift from "in to out" or shore to open waters because then they are ready to turn around and reset more nets all over again. They use the lifter to pull or haul the nets into the boat. The lifter is a simple, hydraulic pulley machine with a motor that winds up the chain and the net. The nets get very heavy when they are full of fish so the lifter helps with the heavy work.

The crew's job is to pick the fish out of the net as it is brought into the boat. They sort the fish by type and size and drop them into different boxes.

Jeff cannot help with the lifts yet because he is too young. But he watches as much as he can so when the time is right he will know what to do and how to take care of the fish.

Jeff's job today is to stay in the pilothouse and watch the radar for other boats or dangers in the water such as big logs or other smaller boats that may not be paying attention. He has to steer the boat if he needs to get out of harm's way or if the boat starts to drift off course. The boat should try to stay in a straight line from the inner buoy to the outer buoy while they are lifting to make it easier and keeps the net from tangling.

Not having someone in the pilothouse to watch for such things can be dangerous. There have been times when no one was in the pilothouse monitoring for other boats and a big 1000 foot laker was very close to them! That was very scary because the big laker would not even know the small fishing boat was there. It would probably not even show up on their radar.

Once the fish are inside the boat, it is time to start cleaning them. If the water is smooth, they can start cleaning on the boat while Jeff or his dad steer the course for port. If the lake is rough, they will wait until they dock before they start cleaning or dressing the fish. To dress a fish, they cut a slit up the fish's belly and scrap out all the material from the inside of the fish. When they clean the fish, they throw them onto a steel table that has a hole on one side. They lay a fish in front of them and scrap the "guts" down the hole. This keeps the fish from rotting or spoiling. Keeping the fish on ice helps stop them from spoiling and keeps them fresh until they process them. When the crew is done cleaning the fish, it is Jeff's job to throw the ice on them while they are in their boxes and to clean up the area by removing the garbage, fish guts, and washing off the cleaning tables.

Boxes of' freshly caught fish that have been gutted and are sitting on ice until they can be taken to the fish plant to be processed.

Dressing the fresh fish on the boat after the day's catch.

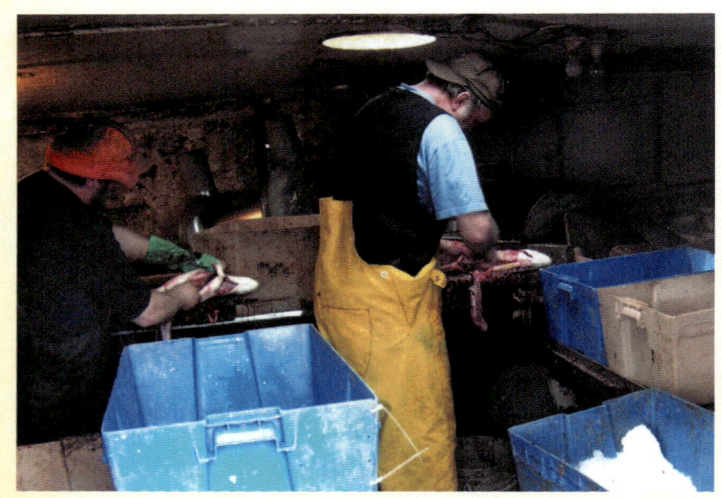

It is about 4:00 in the afternoon. It has been a long, but fun day on the lake. The rest of the crew will haul the fish up to the plant where they will process the fish, now it is time for Jeff to shower and take a long nap. When he wakes up, it will be time to check the fish for ice, eat supper, play a little catch with his dad, and go to bed. Tomorrow is another work day.

Tomorrow, when the rest of the men are on the lake setting more nets, Jeff's job will be to help freeze the fish or sort them into steel barrels to be brined for smoking. He also has to haul in wood to be used in the smoking.

There are three ways the fish are processed. One way is when the fish are given a light coat of glaze to protect them and then laid out to fast freeze. Later, they will be stacked, boxed and labeled for future use. The second way to take the fresh fish or fillets to the local grocery store to be sold. And the third way, is to smoke the fish. This is done in a special building called a smoke house.

One of Jeff's brothers is in charge of smoking the fish. They smoke fish about three to four days a week, depending on how many orders come in to the fisheries. Jeff's dad and grandfather invented a rail system that hangs from the ceiling in their smoke house. This is how they transfer the fish from place to place.

The fish start out in the brine room, move to the smoking room, then to the cooling room, on to the packing room and into a walk-in cooler for storage while waiting to be shipped. The empty racks continue on back to the cleaning room where they will get a good scrubbing.

Fish start here in the brine room. Picture shows stainless barrels being cleaned.

Smoking racks with flat screens. These are used to lay fillets or chunk pieces of fish for smoking

The fish have to sit in a solution called a "brine". This is a salt solution. There is a special formula that they have to use to put the right amount of salt into the water. And there is a lot of paperwork recording all of this information too. The evening before the fish are to be smoked they brine them in big stainless steel barrels with water and salt.

Early the next morning, around 4:00 to 5:00, the brined fish are hung on steel pegs by their tails or laid on a rack if they are slabs or chunks. They are now ready to be smoked.

The racks are gently steered into the smoke room where they enter huge walk-in ovens with real hard wood burning in steel boxes on the floor. The doors are called "Dutch doors" because they are cut in the middle so you can use either the top or bottom or both. The temperature in the oven can be regulated better with this kind of door.

Jeff's brother has to carefully monitor the temperatures in each oven and make sure they stay at a constant temperature for a specific period of time. They use probes and must record times and temperatures. They usually smoke from four to eight ovens a day and three to four days a week. It generally takes about nine hours to smoke all of the fish.

A freshly smoked oven of chubs coming out of the cooler.

A lady is taking the chubs off the pegs and putting them in boxes for retail.

First, they must be weighed, sealed and stamped with dates.

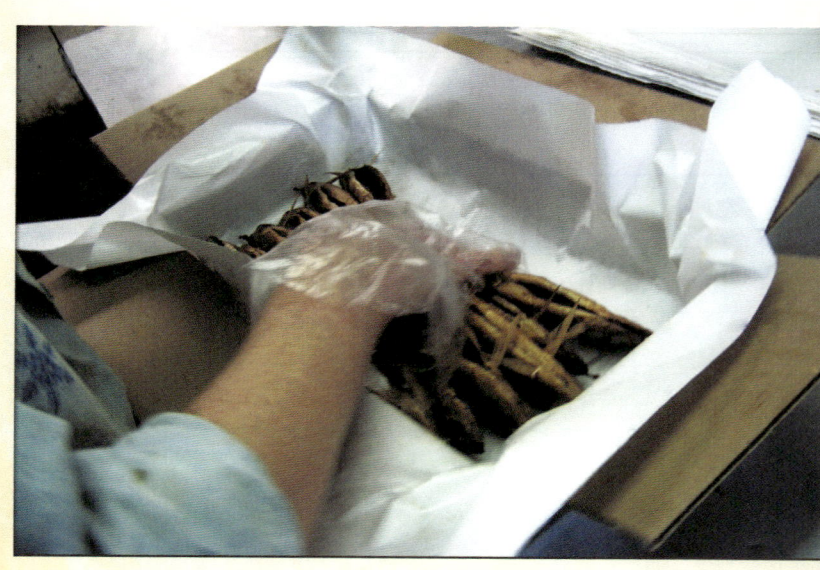

There are three ladies waiting in the packing room to pack off the fish.

They have the list of special orders that came in over the telephone or fax machine so they know how many boxes of fish to pack up for each order.

Every Tuesday and Friday the fresh smoked fish, and maybe some fresh fish, are delivered to various places to be sold. They deliver fresh smoked fish and fresh fish to the local grocery store almost daily.

From mending to setting the fish nets, to lifting and cleaning the fish, to processing by filleting or smoking the fish is a long journey. One that Jeff hopes will be around for a long, long time.

Jeff is the fourth generation of commercial fishermen in his family. He hopes that when he graduates from college he can come back to help his dad and, in time, take over the fishing business.

GLOSSARY

brine = water saturated or nearly saturated with salt that is used as a preservative to stop bacteria. Smoked fish must first be bathed in a salt brine.

buoy = a floating object anchored in a body of water to mark the beginning and ending of a fish net. Each fisherman has his own symbol or color.

chubs = a deepwater fish silvery in color with a greenish tint and grows to about 12 inches. It is used mainly for smoking and bait. The meat is moist.

herring = small, slender silver bodies with pink to purple shades, a relative of the whitefish that lives at different depths depending on the water temperature. They grow to 15 inches. Herring are used as bait, pickled, smoked, and cooked. The meat is drier then chubs.

laker = a large vessel that is used to carry products on the Great Lakes

Lakers carry bulk cargoes of materials such as limestone, iron ore, grain, coal or salt. The largest of these are 1000 feet long.

lifter = a hydraulic machine that is fastened onto the side of a commercial fishing boat used to help pull nets full of fish into the boat.

Nor-easter = called this because the winds come from the northeast. The most frequent and violent are between September and December on the south shore of Lake Superior. They bring rain, winds of gale force and very rough, high seas.

needles = an oblong-shaped piece of plastic that has an opening at one end with nylon thread wrapped around the length of the needle. It is used in mending the ripped fishing nets.

oilers = protective bib-like outwear made out of heavy rubber like material that fishermen wear for protection from weather, water, cleaning gutting fish.

sea lamprey = is an aggressive parasite that attaches itself to the side of a fish, usually trout or whitefish, with its tooth filled round mouth and hangs on until it is full. This usually kills the fish. It looks like an eel, averages 12 to 20 inches and almost a pound. They are an ocean fish that made their way into the Great Lakes through the Welland Canal.

smokehouse = a place where the fish are brined, smoked, and packed for shipping and sale to various places.

Trout (lean) = often referred to as "lakers", they average 17 to 27 inches and weighs about 7 pounds, but can reach weights of 25 pounds. They have lighter spots on a dark background and a light underside. They were once in danger of extinction because of the sea lamprey and over fishing, but because of regulations, stocking, and sea lamprey control they are thriving. They are cooked in many ways, but their meat is oilier than most. These fish have enforced restrictions from the DNR.

trout (fats) = they are the same as a lean trout only much fattier. These are the trophy large trout. They can be eaten also, but are best used in smoking.

whitefish = are silvery with light greenish-brown backs. They live in cold deep waters so are more a commercial fish rather then a sports fish. Their' meat is white and moist. They average 17 to 22 inches and up to 4 pounds. These fish have enforced restrictions from the DNR.

Smoked Chubs (Ciscoes) = freshly caught from Lake Superior by local commercial fishermen, they are considered the gourmet of smoked fish. Smoked chubs are moist and rich with healthy omega-3 fatty acids and HDL cholesterols that help remove arterial blocking substances that cause heart disease. Plus, the hardwood smoke adds an enriching flavor to the fish.

Smoked Herring = Freshly caught from Lake Superior, they have less oils than smoked chubs and therefore have a much drier texture. Because of their abundance, they are the cheaper line of smoked fish.

Smoked Whitefish = are a Lake Superior fish that is also moist and rich with healthy oils and have a hearty flavor because of their bigger size.

Smoked Lake Trout = are the kingpin of healthy fish oils. Lake trout have 2-3 times the oil content of the other fish. They smoke up without drying out.

Fisherman mending net 5 hours a day for many weeks

Boxes of nets to be mended

Oilers worn on boat and fish plants

CPSIA information can be obtained
at www.ICGtesting.com
Printed in the USA
LVIC04n0248030615
440971LV00004B/11